BIBLE 12〇△
THE TRIN

CONTENTS

Author:	**Barry G. Burrus, M.Div, M.A., B.S.**
Editor:	Alan Christopherson, M.S.
Illustrations:	David Sprenger
	Kyle R. Bennett, A.S.

Alpha Omega Publications ®

804 North 2nd Avenue East, Rock Rapids, Iowa 51246-1759
© MM by Alpha Omega Publications, Inc. All rights reserved.
LIFEPAC is a registered trademark of Alpha Omega Publications, Inc.

BIBLE 1204
THE TRINITY

CONTENTS

Author ...

Editor ...

THE TRINITY

In this LIFEPAC®, you will study **The Trinity**. As Christians, we believe in One God revealed to us in Three Persons: Father, Son, and Holy Spirit. This is known as The Trinity or The Holy Trinity, and is perhaps the supreme doctrine of the Christian faith.

By studying how the Old Testament laid the groundwork for the revelation of the Trinity, you will better understand the concept's development in the New Testament and Church history. Reflections on the development of Trinitarian belief will help you to understand the importance of this truth to modern Christians.

OBJECTIVES

Read these objectives. The objectives tell you what you will be able to do when you have successfully completed this LIFEPAC.

When you have finished this LIFEPAC, you should be able to:

1. Describe the Trinity.

2. State the importance of God's revelation about Himself.

3. Describe the extent of the revelation of the Trinity in the Old Testament.

4. Give several names of God in the Old Testament that are used to imply the Trinity.

5. Relate the meaning of the names of God to the study of the Trinity.

6. Explain how the Trinity is revealed in the New Testament.

7. Outline the development of the Church's belief in the Trinity.

8. Discuss the significance of having faith in the Trinity.

9. Apply the teachings to life in society.

Survey the LIFEPAC. Ask yourself some questions about this study. Write your questions here.

_____

_____

_____

_____

_____

_____

_____

_____

_____

_____

I. OLD TESTAMENT

Christians believe in One God revealed in Three Persons. In this section, we shall study the importance, nature, and extent of God's Trinitarian revelation of Himself and His names as found in the Old Testament.

SECTION OBJECTIVES

Review these objectives When you have completed this section, should be able to:

1. Describe the Trinity.
2. State the importance of God's revelation about Himself.
3. Describe the extent of Trinitarian revelation in the Old Testament.
4. Give several names of God in the Old Testament used to imply the Trinity.
5. Relate the names of God to the study of the Trinity.

VOCABULARY

Study these words to enhance your learning success in this section.

Adonai	foreshadow	monotheism
codify	genitive	trinitarian
Elohim (El)	kyrios	Trinity
etymology	Messianic	Yahweh

Note: All vocabulary words in this LIFEPAC appear in **boldface** print the first time they are used. If you are unsure of the meaning when you are reading, study the definitions given.

REVELATION

As Christians, we look to the Bible as the source of God's revelation about Himself. God revealed Himself in the Old Testament as the one, only, living, and personal God who loves and has an ongoing relationship with His people. Since Christians believe the Bible is the source of God's revelation, we look to the Old Testament to see how God slowly but surely began to prepare man for the knowledge of God as Father, Son, and Holy Spirit: the **Trinity**. The Trinity is basic to our faith and is a point of unity among Christians.

Necessity. The Trinity had to be revealed by God Himself in order to be true. In the Old Testament, the foundation and preparation for this belief was established. By firmly establishing **monotheism**, God prepared His people to receive the message of Jesus Christ regarding His nature and identity.

In the Old Testament, God was in constant touch with His people, guiding them by His law to love and to serve Him and each other. They were encouraged to rely on God in all circumstances. Their belief in *one* God set them apart from the pagans, for their neighbors believed in many gods.

The Israelites believed in One God who revealed himself to them through the Patriarchs Abraham, Isaac, and Jacob; through Moses and the Prophets. The Hebrews knew the One, True God, exclusively by His revelation, for they had no other way to learn about Him.

"I WILL BE YOUR GOD; YOU WILL BE MY PEOPLE."

Old Testament. The complete, sudden revelation of the Trinity to the Jewish nation would have been confusing, for the identification with the one God was just being **codified**. The Old Testament clearly distinguishes between the God of Israel, other "gods", and man. However, the individual persons of the Trinity are only foreshadowed in the Hebrew text.

The understanding of a personal, living God, who has a relationship with man, is a vital theme of the Old Testament, for it prepares us to understand the relationships within the Trinity. Although the Old Testament does not fully explain the Trinity, it gives us the words used to distinguish and foreshadow the three Persons. By studying the way God speaks of Himself in the Old Testament, we lay the foundation for the trinitarian understanding of His identity.

Complete these statements.

1.1 The revelation of One God in Three Persons is called _____ .

1.2 The Old Testament brings out the difference between God and other a. _____ and between God and b. _____ .

1.3 A sudden, complete explanation of the Trinity would have _____ the Jewish nation.

1.4 God had to prepare His people to receive the explanation of the Trinity which would come through _____ .

1.5 To learn God's true nature, man needs _____ .

1.6 The Trinity refers to God as a. _____ , b. _____ , and c. _____ .

1.7 The Trinity is _____ to our faith.

1.8 The Trinity is a point of _____ among Christians.

1.9 The Jewish nation believed in God as the _____ , personal, and living God.

1.10 The Old Testament gives us the _____ for the Trinity.

Answer this question in a paragraph.

1.11 Why is revelation important in the study of the Trinity?

_____

_____

_____

_____

_____

_____

_____

Do this activity.

1.12 Attend a regular service of your local church. Note all references to the Father, Son, and/or Spirit in the sermon, prayers, songs etc. Summarize your findings on a separate sheet. Include the frequency, nature, and importance of each reference. Report to your teacher when complete.

NAMES OF GOD

The names of God in the Old Testament allows us to identify Him personally, preparing us for the notion of more than one Person within the Godhead.

Elohim (El). This name is used 2,550 times in the Old Testament. *El* in Hebrew refers to a divine being and is used in the Old Testament to suggest a supreme god. *Elohim* is a plural noun (Genesis 1:1). When Elohim is seen in the light of Christian revelation, we can recognize this name as an early reference to God in multiple Persons. Elohim refers to God and indicates His majesty and power not only over man, but other false "gods" as well.

Israel used the names *El* and *Elohim*, in combination with defining **genitives** to designate Him as their specific God. Examples can be found in Genesis: *El Bethel* (Genesis 35:7); *El* of your fathers (Genesis 49:25); *El* of eternity (Genesis 21:33); *El* the *Elohim* of Israel (Genesis 33:20) and in Psalms: *El* of Jacob (Psalm 146:5), and *El* of Israel (Psalm 68:35).

The **etymology** of *El Elohim* is uncertain, but the meaning is generally understood as power.

YHWH (Yahweh). The most important name for God in the Old Testament is *YHWH*, usually written as "*Yahweh*," the personal name God revealed to Moses in the Burning Bush (Exodus 3:13-15). Various meanings of the name YHWH are "I Am Who I Am" or "I Will Be Who I Will Be." The Hebrew word Yahweh is translated as LORD (notice all capitals) in most Old Testament English translations. The etymology of Yahweh is disputed, most scholars think the name may be derived from the Hebrew verb *hawah*, meaning *to be*. The name characterizes God as a set-apart, eternal Creator who was God of Israel alone; the God of Moses, who personally revealed Himself through the covenant and as One who can keep His covenants. This title occurs about 6,800 times in the Scriptures.

Yahweh as a *Father* is seen strongly in the Old Testament as Father of Israel, the Father of His people. The title Father expresses a loving relationship between God and His people and encourages a loving obedience from them. God takes care of His people, offering them forgiveness and compassion when they are rebellious. Hebrew personal names illustrate that God is considered a Father: *Joab*, for example, means *Yahweh is Father*; *Abeil* or *Eliab* means *El is Father*; *Abitub* means *my father is goodness*; *Abiezer* means, *my father my help*; and *Absalom* means, *my father is peace*. Besides naming God as Father, these names also illustrate His fatherly characteristics.

Adonai. The title *Lord* was used to indicate the kingship of Yahweh. *Adonai* is a form of the Hebrew word *adon* which is used to address Yahweh to distinguish His kingship from that of an earthly lord as is expressed in the Hebrew form *adoni*.

Because of the Israelites' increasing desire to hallow or sanctify God's name, Yahweh, and avoid misusing it, the title *Adonai* was pronounced in its place when reading the Scriptures. The Hebrew Adonai means "My Great Lord." (The English word *Jehovah* is a translation of God's name during the late Middle Ages which attempted to combine of the consonants YHWH and the vowels of Adonai, *a-o-a*, to form a hybrid word.) In the Greek translation of the Old Testament (called the Septuagint), the Greek term **kyrios** appears as a translation of the name Yahweh. Like Adonai, this Greek word also means "Lord." The use of *kyrios* in reference to Jesus in early Christian writings clearly identifies Him as God, the Yahweh, and Adonai of the Old Testament (Acts 11:20-21).

The title Adonai establishes God as the Lord of His people. As Lord, He has a right to expect obedience from His servants. As servants, His people have a right to expect provision from their Lord. This same concept is seen in the New Testament with the title *Kyrios*.

Significance. In the Old Testament, God is revealed as One Divine Being, unique to Israel. Yahweh stands out as the one true *Elohim*, *Adonai*, and divine Lord. Wisdom belongs to Yahweh alone. His Word is powerful and creative, giving life to all. The use of these terms were valuable to preparing the people of God for the full revelation of the

Trinity, because these names are also used for the Messiah. In the New Testament, Jesus is called the *Son* and the *Word of God*.

Though *Son of God* is used in the Old Testament, it is not used as a **Messianic** title. It was first used of heavenly beings, then to the special relationship between Israel's king (2 Samuel 7:14-16) and God, and to His acceptance of the individual Israelite.

Spirit has wide use in the Old Testament as breath, wind, principle of life, and Creator of all life.

 Read Psalms 2 and 22.

Answer the following questions with complete sentences.

1.13   What are the names of God in the Old Testament listed in this LIFEPAC?

_____

_____

_____

1.14   Why are the names of God important in studying the Trinity?

_____

_____

_____

1.15   What is the meaning of *El, Elohim*? _____

_____

1.16   What was unique about Israel's use of the term *El*?

_____

_____

_____

1.17   Why is the use of the name *Yahweh* significant? _____

_____

_____

_____

1.18   What is the derivation of the name Yahweh? What does this meaning reveal about God?

_____

_____

_____

1.19   What does the title *Father* tell us about God? _____

_____

_____

1.20   What is one indication that the Israelites saw Yahweh as a *Father*?

_____

_____

1.21   What is the meaning of *Adonai*? _____

_____

_____

1.22   What is the parallel between *Adonai* and *kyrios*? _____

_____

_____

1.23   What are two usages of Son of God in the Old Testament? Is it a Messianic title?

_____

_____

_____

1.24   What does Spirit signify in the Old Testament? _____

_____

_____

 Complete the following activity.

1.25   Locate the following references in your Bible and read them carefully. In the space provided, tell how the word is used.

Father	Son	Spirit
Genesis 2:24 2 Samuel 7:14 Psalm 68:5; 89:26	Exodus 4:22 2 Samuel 7:14 Job 1:6 Proverbs 3:1	Hosea 4:19 Psalm 139:7 Genesis 1:2; 6:3

a. **Father** _____

_____

_____

b. **Son** _____

_____

_____

c. **Spirit** _____

_____

_____

 Complete this research project.

1.26   Write a 500-word paper to be completed and submitted before going on to Section II. Submit your outline for the next Teacher check and your paper for the one following Self Test 1. Utilize several resources. In your paper, list additional information on the names of God. Find additional compound names. Locate ten Old Testament verses that use one (or more) of the names for God you have studied. Why did God choose to reveal Himself by the name(s) in the passages you found?

Review the material in this section in preparation for the Self Test. This Self Test will check your mastery of this particular section. The items missed on this Self Test will indicate specific areas where restudy is needed for mastery.

SELF TEST 1

Answer *true* **or** *false* (each answer, 1 point).

1.01 _____ The Trinity refers to One God in Three Persons: Father, Son, and Holy Spirit.

1.02 _____ God is seen as impersonal in the Old Testament.

1.03 _____ The Trinity is not fully revealed in the Old Testament.

1.04 _____ Language from the Old Testament is helpful in the study of the Trinity.

1.05 _____ The *El* of Israel was only one of many Elohim as far as the Hebrews were concerned.

1.06 _____ *Yahweh* is derived from the verb *to make*.

1.07 _____ The etymology of all the Old Testament names is certain.

1.08 _____ Yahweh names a personal God.

1.09 _____ The Son of God in the Old Testament is not a divine Person.

1.010 _____ The use of Spirit in the Old Testament does not influence our present meaning.

Choose the correct answer (each answer, 2 points).

1.011 The Trinity in Christian belief is _____ .
   a. One God in Three Persons   c. three Gods
   b. three Natures

1.012 Belief in God as Trinity is _____ .
   a. basic to all religions   c. a unifying factor among Christians
   b. a central belief for the Jews

1.013 In the Old Testament, God _____ .
   a. revealed Himself as three Persons in one God
   b. prepared Israel for the revelation of Jesus
   c. revealed the existence of the Son and the Spirit

1.014 The names of God in the Old Testament _____ .
   a. reveal a personal living God   c. do not appear in the New Testament
   b. reveal the Trinity

1.015 *El, Elohim,* as used in the Old Testament _____ .
   a. refers to a single divine being   c. refers to all heavenly beings
   b. refers to many different gods

1.016 *Yahweh* in the Old Testament _____ .
   a. characterizes God as Father   c. characterizes God as Messiah
   b. characterizes God as Spirit

1.017 *Father* in the Old Testament _____ .
   a. refers to God the Father as a Person of the Trinity
   b. refers to God as the Father of Israel
   c. refers to God as the Father of Jesus

7

1.018   The form *Adonai* was used in the Old Testament _____ .

         a. of all earthly lords and kings to indicate power   c. in place of *kyrios*

         b. to indicate Yahweh's unique kingship

1.019   *Son of God* in the Old Testament _____ .

         a. is a Messianic title   c. refers only to heavenly beings

         b. expresses a special relationship between God and man

1.020   *Spirit* in the Old Testament _____ .

         a. signifies a Person of the Trinity   c. is a Messianic title

         b. is breath, wind, and principle of life

Do these activities (each numbered answer, 5 points).

1.021   List five attributes or actions of God described in this section.

         a. _____

         b. _____

         c. _____

         d. _____

         e. _____

32 / 40

Score
Adult check _____

          Initial   **Date**

Research Project
Adult check _____

          Initial   **Date**

II. NEW TESTAMENT

In the previous section, you studied that Old Testament names of God are used to foreshadow the Persons of the Trinity. In the New Testament, both *Word* and *Son* are used to illustrate Jesus the Messiah, as a Divine Person distinct from the Father. In this section, we will concentrate on the term *Son of God* which takes on a **familial** meaning when applied to Jesus. The focus is on the Trinity as revealed in the Gospels and **Epistles** of Paul through the terms *Father*, *Son*, and *Spirit*.

SECTION OBJECTIVES

Review these objectives When you have completed this section, should be able to:

1. Give information from the synoptic Gospels.
2. Show what is added to the revelation of the Trinity in John's Gospel.
3. Identify the divine Persons as found in Paul's Epistles.
4. Explain the meaning of the revelations in Paul's letters.

VOCABULARY

Study these words to enhance your learning success in this section.

| Epistles | Paraclete | Transfiguration |
| familial | synoptic Gospels | |

THE GOSPELS

God revealed His trinitarian nature more completely in the Gospels than the Old Testament. We will look first at the **synoptic Gospels** and then at the Gospel according to John.

Synoptic Gospels. The Gospels according to Matthew, Mark, and Luke recorded the Word of God as Jesus preached to (sometimes hostile) audiences. The revelation of the Trinity is not as explicit in those Gospels as in the writings of John and Paul, whose audiences were largely Christian. In the Old Testament, we saw how God began to prepare His people for the revelation of Himself as a Trinity. In the New Testament, we see how Jesus, the Son of God, continued the revelation of the Father and prepared His followers to receive the Holy Spirit.

 Read Matthew 6:5-8, 7:11, 10:29-31, 11:25-27, 15:13, 16:17, and 18:14.
Mark 11:25 and 14:35-39.
Luke 2:49, 10:21, 11:13, 15:11-32, and 22:28-30.

Jesus affirmed the Jewish understanding of God's fatherhood and revealed the extent of the Father's love for His people. The Father is shown as the forgiving, perfect father and ultimate authority.

In addition to God as Father to His people, Jesus revealed His own familial relationship with Him. Jesus proclaimed both this closeness, and His own personal divinity in John 10:30 by stating "I and *my* Father are one." The Father and Son can only be known completely by each other, said Jesus, making it clear that the Fatherhood of God is special and unique for Him as His Son.

 Read Matthew 3:17, 4:3, 8:29, 14:33, 16:16, 17:5, and 26:63.
Mark 1:11, 5:7, 3:11, 9:7, and 14:61.
Luke 3:22, 4:3,9, 4:41, 8:28, and 9:35.

The title of "Son of God" is given to Christ throughout the synoptic Gospels by both Jesus Himself and others. In the accounts His Baptism and **Transfiguration**, the Father declared the mission of the Son by using this title. Jesus' unique sonship is clearly indicated in the prediction of the Second Coming and the story of the vinedresser and his son. The passage (Matthew 11:27) shows the exclusive knowledge the Son has of the Father, and vice versa.

 Read Matthew 1:18, 20; 3:13-17; 12:28, 32; 22:43; and 24:20.
Mark 1:9-12, 3:29, 12:36, and 13:11.
Luke 11:20 and 12:10.

Spirit is used in the New Testament much the same as in the Old to signify the principle of life and good actions. However, in the New Testament, *spirit* also connotes the power of God conferred on Jesus and His disciples. Jesus' conception by the Holy Spirit set Him apart as One who had a unique relationship to God. At Jesus' baptism, the Holy Spirit along with the Father, gave authority to Jesus and recognized His obedience.

In Matthew 28:19, the risen Christ told his disciples to baptize in the name of the Father, the Son, and Holy Spirit. This passage is one of the few instances in the synoptic Gospels where all three Persons are named together.

Complete these statements.

2.1 The books, Matthew, Mark, and Luke are called the a. _____ because b. _____ .

2.2 The revelation of the Trinity in the New Testament is _____ than in the Old Testament.

2.3 The audiences for the Gospels of Matthew, Mark, and Luke as Jesus preached to them were sometimes _____ .

2.4 In the New Testament, Christ a. _____ the revelation of the Father and b. _____ believers for the Spirit.

2.5 The Father is shown as the a. _____ and b. _____ .

2.6 Jesus especially reveals the Father's _____ in the story of the prodigal son.

2.7 Jesus' unique relationship with God is revealed by the title _____ .

2.8 The title "Son of God" is given to Jesus by both a. _____ and b. _____ .

2.9 In the accounts of the a. _____ and the b. _____ the title Son of God gives authority to Jesus' mission.

2.10 Jesus' unique sonship is indicated by the *story* of _____ .

2.11 Jesus' unique sonship is indicated in the *prediction* of

_____

2.12 Spirit is used in both the New and Old Testaments. In reference to Christ, *Spirit* connotes

_____

2.13 The Spirit gave authority to Jesus and recognized His _____ .

2.14 A passage in the Synoptic Gospels which names the three Persons can be found in

_____ .

Answer the following question in complete sentences.

2.15 The developing revelation of which Person (Father, Son or Holy Spirit) is most significant to you? Why?

_____

_____

_____

_____

Johannine Gospel. John's Gospel was probably written about 10-30 years later than those of Matthew, Mark or Luke. Since the audience of John's Gospel was, for the most part, believers, he could be more explicit in talking about the Trinity without fear of threatening their faith.

In the Gospel according to John, we see the Father primarily as the Father of Jesus. Jesus' human life and authority come from the Father. Jesus is also revealed more clearly as the divine Son and Word of God.

 Read John 1:14-18, 6:57, 14:6-28, 16:15-23, and 17:21.

The use of *Son of God* in John shows the extended development of trinitarian doctrine. As previously stated, Jesus enjoys a special union with the Father, but he is also the Divine Person, the only one who brings us into fellowship with the Father. He is Messiah, Redeemer, and Son of God by virtue of His deity.

 Read John 3:16-18, 5:19, and 6:40. 1 John 1:3, 2:22-25, 4:9-13, and 5:13.

In John, *Spirit* is understood to be a person in the Trinity. As **Paraclete**, the Holy Spirit continues the work of Jesus in the world as He is sent by God to comfort Christians. The symbolism of breath and the principle of life found in the Old Testament is extended here specifically to the personality of the Holy Spirit.

Read John 1:33, 3:34, chapters 14-16; 1 John 3:24 and 4:13. Answer this question.

2.16   Which Person(s) of the Trinity are mentioned in these passages?

_____

_____

_____

_____

THE TRANSFIGURATION

PAUL'S EPISTLES

Paul's letters were written to Christian churches or individuals to encourage and strengthen them in their faith. Although Paul was originally a Christian-persecuting Jew, he was dramatically converted by a direct revelation of the Risen Christ. From then on, he was a tireless missionary and Apostle, primarily to the Gentiles.

In some passages, Paul makes a direct reference to all three Persons of the Trinity. For example, in 1 Corinthians 12:4-6, Paul refers to the Spirit (the Holy Spirit), the Lord (meaning Jesus), and God (meaning the Father). Paul closes his second letter to the Corinthians with reference to the Lord Jesus Christ, God (the Father), and the Holy Spirit (2 Corinthians 13:14). Although Paul never explicitly wrote the term "Trinity," he did understand that there was One God in three Persons; specifically, the Father, Son, and Holy Spirit.

Identity of the divine Persons. Paul writes about the *Father* as the One who loves us enough to send His Son (by the power of the Holy Spirit) to redeem us. He brings all things back to Himself through Christ.

Paul frequently used the title *Son of God* frequently in his Epistles to mean God's only begotten Son, Jesus Christ. Christ revealed the Father because He is both God's image and God Himself. Jesus is LORD, divine, and glorified in the Father. *LORD* or *Adonai* had previously been used in the Bible only to translate YHWH. By saying that the *LORD* is Jesus, He is identified as God. For Paul, the Resurrection specifically leaves no question of Jesus' divinity.

Paul presents more information on the role and work of the Holy Spirit than found in the Gospels. Through the regenerating work of the Holy Spirit, we are given eternal life. The gifts of the Spirit are from God and necessary to continue the work of Jesus in building up the Church. The linking of the Spirit specifically with Christ in Paul's Epistles prepares Christians for the recognition of the Spirit as a distinct Person.

Significance. Paul's Epistles teach us how to live in Christ (Ephesians 5:1-2) and in the Spirit. Jesus, our Redeemer, is God's only begotten Son, Who existed as God before His Incarnation on the earth. As the redeemed, Christians are to sing praise to God and to worship Him alone.

Complete these activities.

2.17   Read Romans chapter 8. Describe Paul's view of the Trinity as summarized in this passage.

_____

_____

_____

_____

_____

2.18   Why is the use of *Lord* significant in Paul's Epistles?

_____

_____

2.19   Read Galatians 4:4-5. Copy the quotation in this space.

_____

_____

_____

_____

_____

 Review the material in this section in preparation for the Self Test. This Self Test will check your mastery of this particular section as well as your knowledge of the previous section.

BIBLE 1204 LIFEPAC TEST

BIBLE

1 2 0 4

LIFEPAC TEST

70 / 87

Name _____

Date _____

Score _____

BIBLE 1204: LIFEPAC TEST

Answer *true* or *false* (each answer, 1 point).

1. _____ Old Testament information about the Trinity is limited.
2. _____ Paul holds that the Resurrection proves the divinity of Christ.
3. _____ The third century theologians debated the question of the unity of God.
4. _____ Faith in the Trinity has significant practical application.
5. _____ The baptismal creeds do not mention the Trinity.
6. _____ Adoptionism caused a struggle in the second century.
7. _____ Belief in the Trinity is a basis of Christian unity.

Match these items (each answer, 2 points).

8. _____ necessary to learn of existence of Trinity
9. _____ necessary to show Jesus is God
10. _____ necessary to any interaction with the Trinity
11. _____ necessary to divinity of each Person
12. _____ is seen in abiding love between the Divine Persons

a. unity
b. faith
c. equality
d. distinction
e. revelation
f. Resurrection

Choose the correct answer (each answer, 2 points).

13. Names of God in the Old Testament _____ the Trinity.
    a. imply   b. reveal   c. motivate
14. The story of the vinedresser shows Jesus as _____ .
    a. Messiah   b. Redeemer   c. Son of God
15. God revealed Himself to be a _____ .
    a. single Adonai among many   b. trinity of gods   c. Trinity
16. Theologians can show that the Trinity is _____ .
    a. explainable   b. reasonable   c. completely understandable

Complete these statements (each answer, 3 points).

17. The Trinity consists of a. _____ , b. _____ , and c. _____ .
18. John's Gospel teaches that the Father, Son, and Spirit are _____ .
19. Religious rites, hymns, and prayers showed the _____ belief in the Trinity.
20. God the _____ is the Redeemer.
21. Our relationship with the Father is through _____ .
22. The two essential aspects of the Trinity are a. _____ and b. _____ .

Answer these questions (each answer, 5 points).

23.   How does the New Testament describe the Trinity?

_____

_____

_____

_____

24.   What are the specific missions of each Divine Person?

_____

_____

_____

_____

25.   How can you witness to your belief in the Trinity?

_____

_____

_____

_____

Define the following names of God (each answer, 4 points).

26.   El, Elohim   _____

27.   Yahweh   _____

28.   Adonai   _____

29.   Jehovah   _____

30.   Kyrios   _____

NOTES

Write *O* **for Old Testament or** *N* **for New Testament next to each statement to show where the idea is first presented** (each answer, 2 points).

2.01 _____ The Messiah is promised.

2.02 _____ God is called Father.

2.03 _____ The Holy Spirit is given to believers.

2.04 _____ The Father is a specific Person of the Trinity.

2.05 _____ Jesus and the Father are one.

2.06 _____ God is a personal God.

2.07 _____ Heavenly beings called sons of God.

2.08 _____ The Son of God is Jesus the Christ.

2.09 _____ The Word of God is creative and powerful.

2.010 _____ The Word of God is the Son of God.

Complete these statements (each answer, 3 points).

2.011 Some attributes of the Father found in the Gospels are
a. _____ , b. _____ , and c. _____ .

2.012 Jesus reveals His unique relationship with the Father when He says, "I and my Father
_____ ."

2.013 The parable of _____ shows God's forgiveness.

2.014 The vinedresser story brings out _____
_____ .

2.015 Jesus was _____ by the Spirit.

2.016 One incident in Jesus' life that reveals Him as God's Son is _____ .

2.017 Jesus is clearly seen as a divine Person in the Gospel of _____ .

2.018 The Spirit continues the work of Jesus under the name of _____ according to John.

2.019 Jesus qualified to be the Redeemer by virtue of His _____ .

2.020 Jesus' proper name according to Paul is _____ .

Answer *true* **or** *false* (each answer, 1 point).

2.021 _____ The event which Paul felt clearly showed Jesus as divine is the Transfiguration.

2.022 _____ John's and Paul's audiences were predominantly Christians.

2.023 _____ The words for the Trinity are not used in the same way all the time.

2.024 _____ Father, Son, and Spirit are mentioned together many times in the synoptic Gospels.

2.025 _____ The Old and New Testaments are about equal in their revelation of the Trinity.

2.026 _____ *Trinity* refers to the personality of God.

2.027 _____ God is shown in the Old Testament as a personal God.

2.028 _____ *Yahweh* is derived from the verb *to make.*

2.029 _____ *Yahweh* names a personal God.

2.030	_____	The *El* of Israel was only one of many *Elohim*.
2.031	_____	Belief in the Trinity is basic to all religions.
2.032	_____	*Adonai* in the Old Testament is parallel to *kyrios* in the New Testament.
2.033	_____	*Son of God* in the Old Testament is a term used for believers.
2.034	_____	*Spirit* in the Old Testament is a Messianic title.

Write a paragraph to answer the following question (this answer 6 points).

2.035   Why would revelation of the Trinity have posed a threat to the beliefs of ancient Israel?

_____

_____

_____

_____

_____

```
 61
    76
```

Score
Adult check   _____

                 Initial   **Date**

III. CHURCH HISTORY

The doctrine of the Trinity developed and advanced as God's people sought His wisdom. As Jesus promised (John 16:13), the Holy Spirit guided the early church to the truth about God's nature and identity.

The Old Testament tells us that the Living God is Father. The New Testament adds that God is Jesus' Father and He sends Spirit to His People. In this section, you will see how the early church clarified the belief in the Trinity. The struggles and debates of the first few centuries led to the formulation of creeds proclaiming God to be Father, Son, and Holy Spirit.

It is vital to study the history of the Church's trinitarian formulas, not only because the early fathers settled doubts for further generations, but our very redemption itself rests on Christ being God!

SECTION OBJECTIVES

Review these objectives When you have completed this section, should be able to:

1. Relate the struggles of the second century concerning the Trinity.
2. Describe the nature of third century debates.
3. Give evidence of early Christian belief in the Trinity.
4. Explain the arguments that were used against the Trinity.

VOCABULARY

Study these words to enhance your learning success in this section.

adoptionism	heresy	modalism
Arianism	heretic	theologian
Gnostics	Judaizers	

ORIGIN OF TRINITARIAN FORMULAS

In the first centuries of Christianity, there were many attempts to hold together the belief in the unity of God and the Trinity. At times, it was necessary for authentic Christian authors to combat **heretics** who rejected the Trinity. This section will examine some of the second through fourth-century struggles of Church writers and Councils to codify the teaching on the Trinity. During this period, Christians were able to formulate their understanding of God into specific dogmas defining the Trinity.

Second century. The second century Christian writers Justin and Irenaeus had to struggle against those who would even deny the possibility of three Persons in the One God. Justin and Irenaeus couldn't explain specifically how the three Persons in God related to one another, but they made it clear that God in three Persons is the true Christian belief.

Justin, martyred in Rome in 165 A.D., insisted that the existence of the three Persons did not set aside the belief in God as Creator. The invisible Creator is made known by the visible Word, the Son of God who sent the Spirit. Irenaeus, who wrote in the latter part of the second century, referred frequently to the baptismal creed mentioning the

"WE BELIEVE..."

Father, Son, and Spirit. This trinitarian baptismal formula was already well accepted by the middle of the second century. Against the heretical teachings of the **Gnostics**, Irenaeus explicitly upheld the Trinity.

Both authors identified Christ as the Word of God who has the power to bring men to the Father through the Spirit.

However, many Jews found it difficult to accept the teachings on the Trinity because of their concern for the solidarity of their God. The **Judaizers** strongly preached that the Trinity meant the existence of three separate gods, and therefore was an obvious contradiction to revelation, whereas the Gnostics used their own philosophy rather than scripture to explain Jewish and Christian teachings. However, reason alone cannot explain the Trinity.

Third century. Debates in the third century centered on the distinction of the Persons in the Trinity. **Theologians** Tertullian and Hippolytus of Rome fought against **adoptionism** and **modalism**, two dominant third century **heresies**.

Adoptionism states that Jesus was not really the Son of God, but rather a person in whom God's Word dwelled. However, as Paul wrote, redemption could not have taken place if Jesus were not in fact God. God loved us enough to send His only begotten Son, not a human being adopted by Him, to bring the Word.

Modalism attempts to explain everything in terms of God's unity to such an extent that it destroys the separation of Persons. The modalists, or monarchists, claimed that God was only one Person in three different "modes," or "masks," saying the Father *becomes* the Son while under a different mode. The Spirit is either ignored or represented as just another mode of the Father.

While holding to the unity of God's nature, Tertullian and Hippolytus reaffirmed the Trinity as three Persons in one God and attempted to describe the relationships among the Trinitarian Persons. Hippolytus also enriched the Trinitarian understanding of the baptismal rite. Each Person of the Trinity, though distinct, is divine and equal to the others.

Early Christian prayers and hymns give praise to the Father, Son, and Holy Spirit. Such praise is evidence that the distinction of Persons was even then, in the early Church, a matter of general belief.

Do these activities.

3.1   Name two second-century theologians of the Trinity.

a. _____ and b. _____

3.2   Name two third-century theologians of the Trinity.

a. _____ and b. _____

3.3   Give two evidences of early Christian belief in the Trinity.

a. _____ and b. _____

3.4   Name two groups who preached against the Trinity in the second century.

a. _____ and b. _____

3.5   Name two heresies against the Trinity in the third century.

a. _____ and b. _____

3.6   What two Trinitarian positions did the theologians have to struggle against in the early church?

a. _____ and

b. _____

3.7   What are two reasons why it's important to study the early church's development of trinitarian doctrine?

a. _____

b. _____

Do this project.

3.8   Obtain a copy of the baptismal rite or doctrine of your denomination, or speak with your pastor or church leader about baptism. What does it mention about the Trinity?

_____

_____

3.9   Compare your findings about your baptismal rite with those of a classmate. What conclusions can be drawn?

_____

_____

_____

THE NICENE CREED

By the fourth century, persistent heresies challenging the equality of Persons in the Trinity made it necessary for a specific creed to be declared as Christian dogma. Therefore, the Trinity was clarified in the Nicene Creed.

Attacks against the Trinity. Arius, a theologian from Alexandria in Egypt founded **Arianism**, which denies the equality of Persons in the Trinity. It attracted many followers during the fourth century. He held that the Son could not be coeternal with the Father without threatening monotheism. They held that the Father alone is truly God, the Son is a creation, and the Spirit is not a coeternal person.

The arguments against the Trinity had by this time took three forms: denial of the Trinity altogether; denial of the *distinction* of Persons; and denial of the *equality* of Persons of the Trinity.

Defenses. The theologians of the time tried to develop a common language to explain the nature of God and the relationships within the Trinity. Finally, a Council of Church leaders was held in Nicea (in modern Turkey) in 325 A.D. specifically to refute the Arian heresy. The Council of Nicea gave its approval to a formulation of a Creed that upheld the Son as being coeternal with (and of the same substance as) God the Father. Because of continuing controversy in the fourth century,

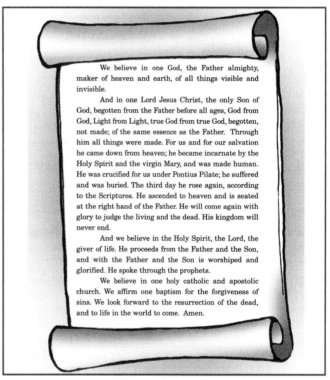

We believe in one God, the Father almighty, maker of heaven and earth, of all things visible and invisible.

And in one Lord Jesus Christ, the only Son of God, begotten from the Father before all ages, God from God, Light from Light, true God from true God, begotten, not made; of the same essence as the Father. Through him all things were made. For us and for our salvation he came down from heaven; he became incarnate by the Holy Spirit and the virgin Mary, and was made human. He was crucified for us under Pontius Pilate; he suffered and was buried. The third day he rose again, according to the Scriptures. He ascended to heaven and is seated at the right hand of the Father. He will come again with glory to judge the living and the dead. His kingdom will never end.

And we believe in the Holy Spirit, the Lord, the giver of life. He proceeds from the Father and the Son, and with the Father and the Son is worshiped and glorified. He spoke through the prophets.

We believe in one holy catholic and apostolic church. We affirm one baptism for the forgiveness of sins. We look forward to the resurrection of the dead, and to life in the world to come. Amen.

THE NICENE CREED

another Council was held in Constantinople in 381 A.D. This Council of Constantinople upheld and reaffirmed the teachings of the Council of Nicea and added clarity to the role of the Holy Spirit. The outcome of these two fourth-century Church councils was an important document known as the *Niceno-Constantinopolitan* or *Nicene Creed*.

OLD TESTAMENT	NEW TESTAMENT	NICENE CREED	
God is living God is Father	God is Father of Jesus Jesus is Son of God Father and Son send Sprit	Godhead	Father Son Spirit

It greatly clarifies for all time the Christian belief in the Trinity: One God as three distinct Persons with one nature, each separate, divine, and equal to the other two.

In the centuries following the declaration of the Nicene Creed, theologians strove to show how the Trinity could be a reasonable, though humanly unexplainable belief.

Answer these questions with complete sentences.

3.10   Why did the Arians reject the Trinity? _____

_____

_____

3.11   What arguments were used against the Trinity?

_____

_____

_____

_____

3.12   Before the Nicene Creed could have been written, what needed to be developed among theologians?

_____

3.13   How was the force of dogma given to the Trinitarian formula?

_____

_____

3.14   What are the main points of Trinitarianism?

_____

3.15   Historically, how have theologians approached the Trinity?

_____

_____

_____

_____

3.16   Why is the emphasis on the divinity of the Spirit important?

_____

_____

_____

_____

Complete this research project.

3.17   Write a 500-word paper to complete and submit before continuing. Submit your outline for the next Teacher check and your paper itself for the one following Self Test 3. Use numerous sources for completing your research. Find the names of the Church fathers, Apologists, Theologians, and Latin fathers in the first through sixth centuries. Some were mentioned in Section III. Find out what they said about God, His Person, and the Trinity. Are they different than the ones mentioned in this LIFEPAC? Compare them.

Review the material in this section in preparation for the Self Test. This Self Test will check your mastery of this particular section. The items missed on this Self Test will indicate specific areas where restudy is needed for mastery.

SELF TEST 3

Match these items (each answer, 2 points).

3.01 _____ thought the Trinity meant more than one God

3.02 _____ tried to explain the faith by philosophy

3.03 _____ said that the Son was a creation

3.04 _____ taught that the Son was a different form of the Father

3.05 _____ taught that the Word only dwelled in Jesus

a. modalism
b. Gnostics
c. adoptionism
d. Arianism
e. Judaizer
f. monotheism

Choose the correct answer (each answer, 2 points).

3.06 One reason theologians hold to the truth of the Trinity is that _____ .
   a. the Old and New Testaments were clear in the revelation of the three Persons
   b. early Christians had professed belief in Father, Son, and Spirit
   c. they had developed a common language about the Trinity

3.07 Justin taught that the Creator _____ .
   a. is the same Person as the Son   c. is not the one God
   b. is made known by the visible Word

3.08 Irenaeus taught that _____ .
   a. the Son is not coeternal with the Father
   b. there is only one Person in God
   c. the baptismal creed indicates three Persons

3.09 Tertullian wrote against _____ .
   a. those who rejected the distinction of Persons
   b. those who accepted the Trinity
   c. those who identified Christ as the Word

3.010 Word in the New Testament _____ .
   a. was used to name Jesus   c. designated the Holy Spirit
   b. was not a Messianic title

3.011 Jesus revealed His unique relationship with the Father by saying that _____ .
   a. He is the Word of God   c. the Father sends the Spirit
   b. He and the Father are one

3.012 Hippolytus wrote _____ .
   a. to counteract the Gnostics   c. to counteract the modalists
   b. to counteract the Arians

3.013 The Trinity is fully known in _____ .
   a. the Old Testament   c. the Bible
   b. all religions

3.014 Theologians can explain _____ .
    a. how the Trinity exists in itself
    b. how the Trinity is a reasonable possibility
    c. how the Trinity can be understood in human terms

3.015 The enumeration of Father, Son, and Spirit _____ .
    a. occurs frequently in the Old Testament   c. occurs frequently in Arian teaching
    b. occurs frequently in the baptismal creed

3.016 One problem with the Trinity took the form of _____ .
    a. questioning the fatherhood of God   c. questioning the authority of Scripture
    b. questioning the unity of God

3.017 The Gnostics and the Judaizers _____ .
    a. accepted Jesus as Son of God   c. accepted the idea of one God
    b. accepted only two Persons in God

3.018 The Apostle Paul tells us our redemption depends on _____ .
    a. Jesus being the Son of God   c. the Spirit being divine
    b. God being three Persons

3.019 Arianism was against _____ .
    a. the fatherhood of God   c. the equality of Persons
    b. the human nature of Christ

Complete these statements (each answer, 3 points).

3.020 One idea present in the Old Testament, New Testament, and Nicene Creed is that God is
_____ .

3.021 New Testament writers who taught Christians about the Father, Son, and Spirit as Persons
are a. _____ and b. _____ .

3.022 Adoptionism and modalism were considered _____ in the early church.

3.023 Each person of the Trinity is a. _____ , b. _____ , and c _____ .

Answer *true* **or** *false* (each answer, 1 point).

3.024 _____ Trinity refers to One God in Three Persons.
3.025 _____ God is seen as impersonal in the Old Testament.
3.026 _____ The Trinity is not fully revealed in the Old Testament.
3.027 _____ Language from the Old Testament is helpful in studying the Trinity.
3.028 _____ The El of Israel was only one of many Elohim as far as the Hebrews were concerned.
3.029 _____ Yahweh is derived from the verb *to make*.
3 030 _____ The etymology of the Old Testament names is certain.
3.031 _____ Yahweh names a personal God.
3.032 _____ The Son of God in the Old Testament is not a divine Person.
3.033 _____ The use of Spirit in the Old Testament does not influence our present meaning.
3.034 _____ The event which Paul felt clearly showed Jesus as divine is the Transfiguration.
3.035 _____ Paul's writings were primarily written to Christians.

3.036   _____ The words for the Trinity are not used in the same way all the time.

3.037   _____ Father, Son, and Holy Spirit are mentioned together by name only once in the synoptics.

3.038   _____ The Old and New Testaments are equal in their revelation of the Trinity.

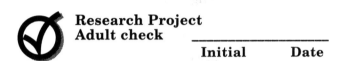

$$\frac{59}{74}$$

Score
Adult check   _____
                Initial   **Date**

Research Project
Adult check   _____
             Initial   **Date**

IV. PRACTICAL IMPLICATIONS

How does the reality of the Trinity affect you? The answer is through Jesus Christ, the way, truth, and life. Jesus, the Son of God, fully divine, and fully human, (through the Holy Spirit) is the only accessway to the Father.

SECTION OBJECTIVES

Review these objectives When you have completed this section, should be able to:

1. Analyze the implications of divine unity.
2. Distinguish the missions of the divine Persons.
3. Apply Trinitarian teachings to life in human society.

VOCABULARY

Study these words to enhance your learning success in this section.

contemplation	impetus	motivate
hallmark	mission	

THE CHURCH

As a **hallmark** of Christianity, belief in the Trinity gives **impetus** to the Christian desire for unity. In studying the **missions** of the divine Persons, we see what our own mission is.

Divine unity. God did not save us and leave us on our own to figure out what to do with ourselves. In His Son, He has given us the focus of our unity, with the Trinity as the perfect example. The Father gives Himself totally to the Son, and the Son returns that love in obedience. The Holy Spirit empowers Christ to express His obedience to the Father.

For all God's people to be unified in abiding love, as the Trinity is, is one of the goals of Christianity. Christians have differed throughout the course of history, but the Trinity has remained a unifying belief.

Divine diversity. The unity of God is just as significant as His diversity.

God the Father loves and gives Himself to His Son and His Creation. He reveals Himself through His Creation and Word, exposing sin and conversely, salvation in Christ. Christians must exhibit the love, creativity, compassion, and forgiveness of the Father.

God the Son redeems us and gives us access to the Father. Christ fulfilled His father's will completely through His perfect fulfillment of the law's demands, sacrificial death, and Resurrection. He thus shows God's love for us. We must exhibit the same to the fallen world.

God the Holy Spirit is sent by both the Father and Son to be a comfort to Christians while Christ is seated at the Father's right hand. Jesus promised that the Spirit would be sent to dwell within us, guide us, and teach us (John 14:26; 15:26 and 16:8-16). He also gives us gifts to be used to build up and renew both the Church and the world.

 **Answer** *true* **or** *false*.

4.1 _____ After Creation, the work of the Father was over.

4.2 _____ Impetus for building unity comes from the example of the Trinity.

4.3 _____ Belief in the Trinity is characteristic of Christianity.

4.4 _____ Christians have no room for differences.

4.5 _____ God's Word reveals God's will.

4.6 _____ Jesus is the Son of God.

4.7 _____ The Trinity is a perfect human unity.

4.8 _____ Christians are expected to form divine unities.

4.9 _____ The Persons of the Trinity do not have individual missions.

4.10 _____ Christians should witness the forgiveness in Jesus Christ to the world.

4.11 _____ The Son is a living testimony to the love of the Father for the world.

4.12 _____ Redemption is the work of the Spirit.

THE INDIVIDUAL

Christians find strength and love by **contemplating** the Trinity.

Christian Life. The living God revealed Himself to the Jewish nation as recorded in the Old Testament, but He reveals Himself perfectly in Jesus as chronicled in the New Testament. He maintains His presence with every child of His throughout all time.

For us to grow spiritually, we must obey His commandments. If we are Christ's disciples, we must behave like we are. Love God with all your heart, soul, mind, and strength. Love all others as you love yourself.

Church Life. What then can we learn from this study of the Trinity that will **motivate** us to better the human community? Understand yourself by understanding God first. Unite together in love with your fellow believers. Live in service for others, and in doing so fulfill the command of Christ.

Answer these items.

4.13 What is the value of personal faith in the Trinity?

_____

_____

_____

4.14 How are we linked with the Trinity?

_____

_____

_____

_____

_____

4.15 How does contemplation of the Trinity motivate us to build unity? _____

_____

_____

_____

_____

Before you take this last Self Test, you may want to do one or more of these self checks.

1. _____ Read the objectives. Determine if you can do them.

2. _____ Restudy the material related to any objectives that you cannot do.

3. _____ Use the SQ3R study procedure to review the material:
   a. **S**can the sections.
   b. **Q**uestion yourself again (review the questions you wrote initially).
   c. **R**ead to answer your questions.
   d. **R**ecite the answers to yourself.
   e. **R**eview areas you didn't understand.

4. _____ Review all activities and Self Tests, writing a correct answer for each wrong answer.

SELF TEST 4

Answer *true* **or** *false* (each answer, 1 point).

4.01 _____ Christian faith in the Trinity is insignificant.

4.02 _____ The Trinity motivates us to be creative.

4.03 _____ God is a Trinity of natures.

4.04 _____ The mission of the Father is to die to redeem us.

4.05 _____ The Jewish nation fully understood the revelation of the Trinity.

4.06 _____ Paul's letters did not mention the Spirit.

4.07 _____ Our redemption depends on Christ's relationship with the Father.

4.08 _____ The Judaizers denied the Trinity as a threat to monotheism.

Choose the correct answer (each answer, 2 points).

4.09 A significant factor in the belief that we are designed to live in unity is that _____ .

  a. all Persons of the Trinity live in abiding love amongst themselves

  b. the Persons of the Trinity have individual missions

  c. Christians must always agree

4.010 God revealed the Trinity _____ .

  a. after careful preparation of His people   c. as the Father of Israel

  b. through the prophets

4.011 The following item was *not* often cited as evidence for an early Christian belief in the Trinity: _____ .

  a. the baptismal creed   c. prayers and hymns

  b. the synoptic Gospels

4.012 John identified the Spirit as _____ .

  a. the Word   c. the Paraclete

  b. the Wisdom of God

4.013 Human unity may be patterned after the divine unity because _____ .

  a. the Father intervenes directly in our lives   c. the Spirit empowers believers to do so

  b. the Son is called the Word of God

4.014 Third-century theologians debated _____ .

  a. the distinction of the Persons   c. the unity of the Persons

  b. the equality of the Persons

4.015 One goal of Christianity is _____ .

  a. to be united in love as the Trinity is   c. to combat worldliness

  b. to eliminate all differences among people

Complete these statements (each answer, 3 points).

4.016 God is a community of Persons eternally co-_____ and abiding in love.

4.017 Two names of God from the Old Testament are a. _____ and b. _____ .

4.018 Our union with God is made possible by _____ .

24

4.019   The Nicene Creed proclaims that each Person of the Trinity is distinct, equal, and

                _____ .

4.020   To reveal the Father is the mission of the _____ .

4.021   The key to having any relationship with the Trinity is _____ .

4.022   The unity which bonds all those who believe in the Trinity is _____ .

4.023   The Trinity had to be proclaimed as a matter of faith because of the _____
        early centuries.

4.024   A relationship with the Father requires _____ .

4.025   Jesus is clearly seen as a divine Person in the Gospel of _____ .

4.026   The Spirit continues the work of Jesus under the name of _____ in John.

4.027   Jesus is able to be the Redeemer by virtue of His _____ .

4.028   Jesus' proper name according to Paul is _____ .

Answer *true* **or** *false* (each answer, 1 point).

4.029   _____   *Trinity* refers to One God in Three Persons.

4.030   _____   God is seen as impersonal in the Old Testament.

4.031   _____   The Trinity is not fully revealed in the Old Testament.

4.032   _____   Language from the Old Testament is helpful in the study of the Trinity.

4.033   _____   The *El* of Israel was only one of many *Elohim* as far as the Hebrews were concerned.

4.034   _____   *Yahweh* is derived from the verb *to make*.

4.035   _____   The etymology of the Old Testament names is certain.

4.036   _____   *Yahweh* names a personal God.

4.037   _____   Son of God in the Old Testament is not used to describe a divine Person.

4.038   _____   The use of Spirit in the Old Testament does not influence our present meaning.

Write a paragraph for each of the following items (each answer, 6 points).

4.039   How do we know that there are three Persons in one God?

    _____

    _____

    _____

    _____

4.040   Why did the teachings on the Trinity get more explicit as time went on?

    _____

    _____

    _____

Before you take the LIFEPAC Test, you may want to do one or more of these self checks.

1. ____ Read the objectives. Determine if you can do them.
2. ____ Restudy the material related to any objectives that you cannot do.
3. ____ Use the SQ3R study procedure to review the material.
4. ____ Review all activities and Self Tests, and LIFEPAC Glossary.
5. ____ Restudy areas of weakness indicated by the last Self Test.

GLOSSARY

Adonai. The Hebrew noun translated as Lord in the Old Testament.

adoptionism. The heresy that Jesus was only an adopted son and therefore not equal to the Father.

Arianism. Named after Arius, a theologian of the fourth century who claimed that Jesus was a creation and that the Holy Spirit was not divine.

codify. To systematize, clearly define.

contemplation. Thinking about something for a long time.

Elohim. A Hebrew plural noun used for the God of Israel.

Epistles. Letters; used to identify the letters of the Apostles in the New Testament.

etymology. The study of the origin and history of words.

familial. Of, or pertaining to a family.

foreshadow. To present an indication or suggestion beforehand.

genitive. In the Hebrew, words which define a nominative.

Gnostics. A false Christian group which believed philosophy (not scripture) is the standard of truth.

hallmark. A mark or sign of genuineness or good quality.

heresy. An opinion or doctrine at variance with established religious beliefs.

heretic. A person who holds opinions or doctrines on any subject contrary to those that are authoritative.

impetus. A driving force.

Judaizers. False Christians who insisted that monotheism excluded the possibility of the Trinity.

kyrios. A Greek noun translated *lord*.

Messianic. Having to do with predictions concerning the Messiah.

mission. A duty.

modalism. Refers to the theory that the one God appears under numerous, different forms.

monotheism. Belief in one God.

motivate. To stimulate to action.

Paraclete. *One called to help*; the Holy Spirit.

synoptic Gospels. The first three Gospels, presenting accounts from the same point of view (i.e., "syn-optic")

theologian. One who studies the nature of God.

trinitarian. Having to do with trinity.

Trinity. One God in three Persons.

Transfiguration. The sudden radiance appearing from Jesus' person while he prayed on the mountain.

YHWH (Yahweh). An Old Testament name for God which emphasizes His promise to keep covenants.